Northumberland National Park
boundary sign

Introduction

In Northumberland alone, both heaven and earth are seen; we walk all day on long ridges, high enough to give far views of moor and valley and the sense of solitude above the world below, It is the land of the far horizons.

'hese words, written by G. M. 'revelyan in 1926, capture the ssence of Northumberland. Al- hough written two decades efore the 1949 Act of Parliament vhich created National Parks, it ells why the hill land of North- mberland, along with nine other reas in England and Wales, was elt to have special importance o the nation. On 5 June 1956 Jorthumberland was the ninth 'ark to be designated, and its laim to be one of the finest andscapes in England and Wales vas officially recognised.

With designation comes the ational Park Authority's statu- ory duty: to protect the land- cape of the Park and to provide ccess to it. The land within the 'ark is not nationalised; it is wned by the people who live in

it and farm it. Beyond this, it has a greater value in its beauty and the benefit people can derive from getting out into it, and relaxing in quiet and far-away places. It is a fine concept and members of Professor Trevelyan's family were in the forefront of the people who worked so hard, more than fifty years ago, to achieve it.

Northumberland National Park covers 1030 square kilometres; in area it is one of the larger parks. It has, however, the smallest num- ber of inhabitants; roughly 2000 people live in it. From the Cheviots in the north, through Coquetdale, Redesdale, North Tynedale and Hadrian's Wall Area, all traversed by the Pennine Way, the population is almost equally sparse because the Park boundary was designed to ex- clude the larger villages and towns.

It is hill farming country, rear- ing both sheep and beef cattle, but there are two exceptions. The Forestry Commission and the Ministry of Defence each own

one fifth of the Park. The Redes- dale All Arms Training Area is the largest range used by NATO forces. The land within it is still farmed and the Ministry of De- fence plays an important role in the conservation of landscape on the range. Because of the danger from live firing, however, there is necessarily a large area of the Park which is accessible to the public only when firing is not taking place (denoted by the absence of red flags) and at lambing time, from 15 April to 15 May each year. Since some of the finest landscape in the Park is on the range, it is worth taking advantage of this annual lull in training procedures. The walker is strictly adjured to keep to public rights of way, however, as the Army do not ensure clearance of live ammunition other than on these routes.

The Forestry Commission has created, in Kielder Forest, the largest forest planted in Europe this century. Parts of Coquetdale and the Cheviots are also heavily planted. This, more than anything else, has changed the character of Northumberland's landscape.

The village of Stonehaugh was built by the Forestry Commission to house forest workers during the rapid growth in planting after World War II. The other villages in the Park are much older settle- ments; clusters of compact grey houses built round a church or fortification. Kirknewton, Alwin- ton, Harbottle, Holystone, Roch- ester, Elsdon and Falstone, all have their roots deep in the past.

The curlew is the symbol of Northumberland National Park. Its distinctive beak, and mournful cry resting on the air as it flies with widespread wings over the moors, were felt to epitomise the solitary nature of this high land.

This booklet describes the geology, local and natural history of the Park, its folk tales and customs. If you have heard the mournful cry of the curlew, imagine too the mournful skirl of the Northumbrian pipes as an accompaniment to your reading.

Hadrian's Wall Area

Just when you think you are at the world's end, you see smoke from East to West as far as the eye can turn, and then, under it, also as far as the eye can stretch, houses, temples, shops and theatres, barracks and granaries, trickling along like dice behind – always behind – one long, low, rising and falling, and hiding, and showing, line of towers. And that is the Wall!

Puck of Pook's Hill
Rudyard Kipling

It is Hadrian's Wall, built on top of the high natural barrier of the great Whin Sill, which dominates the area. The Romans were here for about 300 years, and the Wall is the most impressive and romantic of their legacies in this country. But it was Julius Agricola, Governor of Britain from AD 78 to 84, who first penetrated this far north.

The Stanegate

Agricola overran all the north of England and swept on into Scotland. His policy was to build forts throughout the north, linking them with stone roads. The Stanegate, in this area, linked Corbridge with Carlisle. The Stanegate fort of Vindolanda has a superb *vicus*, or civil settlement and north of the fort, close to the farm of Codley Gate, is a milestone, one of only two which are still intact and in their original position.

Hadrian's Wall

Sporadic unrest among the northern Britons erupted in the first year of the Emperor Hadrian's reign, AD 117, into a full-scale rising. Hadrian came to Britain to see what needed to be done and he ordered the construction of a wall across the narrow neck of

Hadrian's Wall was not just a barrier; it was also a frontier system consisting of a wall, eight to ten feet broad, fifteen feet high with a six-foot-high battlement. There was a ditch on the north as added protection. On the line of the wall were mile-castles to house the patrols and for customs and passport control; turrets, two between each mile-castle, were probably watch-towers; the forts housed much larger bodies of fighting men, both cavalry and infantry. The stone-made Military Way linked all these fortifications, the length of the Wall. The Vallum, a huge ditch with earth mounds each side, marked the southern boundary of the military zone.

Above: Hadrian's Wall from Cuddy's Crags. Far left: Walkers on Hadrian's Wall. Left: Hadrian's Wall at Walltown

Above: The Granary, Housesteads. Opposite, top left: The Bath House at Chesters Port. Opposite, top right: Remains of Mithraic Temple at Brocolitia. Right: Section through Whin Sill at Cawfields Quarry, Hadrian's Wall

land between the Solway Firth and Wallsend on Tyne; seventy-three miles of continuous barrier to separate Rome from the barbarians. The best preserved section lies within the National Park. The Emperor did not stay to see the Wall built. Its construction was supervised in its early stages by Aulus Platorius Nepos, Legate of Britain

Within and around the forts can be found almost every aspect of Roman life. Housesteads Fort contains the Headquarters building, barracks, the CO's quarters, granaries, strongroom, workshops, water tanks, and also the only example of a Roman hospital in Britain as well as a lavatory with flushing tank. Outside the walls were the shops, taverns, temples, houses and the type of civilian settlement that develops alongside any well-established military set-up. The bath houses were always outside the fort's wall; the most impressive one is at Chesters. Close to Carrawburgh are the remarkable remains of a Mithraic temple.

The Whin Sill

This is the great natural feature of the landscape. Formed of dolerite, the sill intruded itself in a molten state between the layers of softer limestone, sandstone, shales and coal, and now forms the crests of the Whin Sill ridge on which the Wall is built. Ice Age erosion had little effect on the hard, north-facing escarpment of the sill, except where softer stone in places allowed the meltwater to force its way through; this is apparent every so often along the ridge where 'gaps' occur, for example at Caw Gap, Rapishaw Gap and Busy Gap. These have provided, to this day, the only easy routes across the Whin Sill.

Commercial Uses

The Romans used sandstone, whinstone and lime, possibly even coal. Sandstone outcrops regularly in this area and was cut for all the facing stones on the Wall and their buildings. Roman grafitti on Barcombe Fell pinpoints one of their quarries. Later builders quarried the Roman works as well as the local out-

Below: Black-face Rams. Opposite, main picture: Crag Lough. Inset: The lovely Bog Asphodel, to be found in the Forest of Lowes

crops for their own houses. Coal-mining was responsible for the growth of Greenhead into a prosperous village in the nineteenth century and three drift mines are still worked in the area.

In the last hundred years two whinstone quarries were worked to make paving setts, or cobblestones, and later for general road-building materials. Both quarries, Walltown and Cawfields, have closed and are now owned by the National Park. Cawfields has been made into a picnic area and car park.

For a long time lime was burnt in small quantities to improve sour or acid soil. With the development of the South Tyne Railway which improved transport, lime was produced commercially as a fertiliser, as the number of limekilns in the area testify. These are always built into a hillside, close to deposits of both lime and coal which were tipped into a hole at the top of the kiln and, after burning, the resultant mixture was raked out at the bottom.

The Forest of Lowes

This area of boggy land north of the Whin Sill did at one time support tree growth, but in reality the Forest was an area of rough grazing land. Wide patches of

raised blanket bog have evolved, ousting tree growth in the period since the last Ice Age and in the Hadrian's Wall Area now there are several Sites of Special Scientific Interest (SSSIs). They may look like waste land, but examined closely, they reveal a rich plant life. The white, fluffy heads of the cotton grass are the most obvious sign of boggy ground. Sphagnum moss, much sought for lining hanging-baskets, covers much of the inhospitable peat, but look closer and a sundew, that traps and feeds on insects, might be found. The lovely bog asphodel, the aromatic bog myrtle and Andromeda, the bog rosemary, are also indicative of damp or boggy ground.

Peat has been used for centuries as a domestic fuel; now it is extracted on quite a large scale for use in horticulture. A much bigger threat to the continued existence of upland mires, however, is afforestation and drainage of land. The National Park can save such important wildlife habitats by compensating farmers for loss of agricultural earnings through non-improvement of the land.

There was a time, however, when these mires or 'mosses' were viewed with a less kindly eye; they gave their name to the term 'moss trooper' – a freebooter or cattle thief, and bands of such people infested these mosses beyond the reach of the law. They were safe because, like the Picts before them harassing the Romans, and the sheep who graze there, they knew the safe ways across the mosses, unlike those in pursuit who, if they missed their footing were likely also to lose their lives.

Farming

The farms in the Hadrian's Wall Area are quite small and are concerned chiefly with sheep rearing – black face and cheviots for the most part. The number of stells (folds) for protecting the stock and the creeps constructed in the drystone walls (even in the Wall itself) to let the sheep through from one pasture to another show how important they are.

Stone walls are a particularly important feature of this landscape and in recent years the National Park has been able to help farmers keep walls in good repair by employing local craftsmen to rebuild sections, or mend them, and by giving financial assistance to this work.

One of the rarer sights on the hills are the blue-grey cattle. Pure-bred galloways, which are quite black, used to be raised but the galloway is now crossed with a shorthorn white bull to get the blue-grey stock. They are a slow-growing type, but very hardy and able to lie out where other cattle would perish.

The number of farms in this area with the word 'shield' incorporated in the name, Shield on the Wall, for example, or Sewingshields, shows that these were the summer pastures for people living in the valley who brought their livestock up here for the summer. The small huts in which they lived while they tended their stock were called shields.

Castles and Towers

The numerous battlements that can be seen stretching along the South Tyne Valley are not the romantic survival of Arthurian England, although Arthur and Guinevere are supposed to have held court up here; witness the King's Crags and Queen's Crags at Sewingshields. Indeed the whole of King Arthur's court is supposed to live entranced in a cave beneath Sewingshields Castle. The castles of Thirlwall, Blenkinsopp, Willimoteswick, Featherstone and Langley, and others that have completely disappeared, were built as very necessary defences in the long period of war with Scotland and later widespread lawlessness. Such was the despair of those trying to keep order on the Border that one of them suggested the Pictes Wall, as Hadrian's Wall was called then, be fortified once again and made into the frontier with Scotland. Northumberland, north of the Wall, could be given to the Scots with few regrets. There was no response.

Shallow lakes or 'loughs', never more than about eleven feet deep, are pools of water lying in depressions caused by glacial erosion during the last Ice Age. Crag Lough (above), Greenlee, Broomlee and Grindon loughs (pronounced 'loff') have gradually grown smaller as organic matter has been deposited in the water by the loughside vegeta-tion; this has accumulated and risen above the water-level so that, in turn, is able to bear water-loving shrubs and trees such as willow. Grindon Lough, which is managed as a nature reserve by the Northumbria Wildlife Trust, almost dries up during hot summers and cows stand in the remaining pools to keep cool.

The Military Road

During the 1745 Jacobite Rebellion, General Wade tried to intercept Bonnie Prince Charlie at Carlisle but was unable to get further than Hexham because no road was strong enough to take his artillery. By Act of Parliament, 1751, the road planned by Wade was allowed to be built and the Military Road (B6318) or Wade's Road, is the result. One result of that road being built is the total lack of much of Hadrian's Wall because it either disappeared under the road or contributed raw material to its building. The stretch in the National Park is well preserved because Wade took the only sensible route there and built the road a hundred yards lower than the crags on level ground.

Plants

The varied soil conditions in Hadrian's Wall Area enable a wide range of plants to grow. Wild thyme lies in thick patches, giving off an aromatic scent when crushed. Bird's-foot trefoil sparkles yellow in the grass; lady's mantle with beads of moisture on its leaf tips and the rock rose shelter in the lea of the Wall. Cowslip, a classic plant of old pastures also grows here. Herb Robert and ragged robin grow in the lower, damper ground. The wild chive survives on Walltown Crags; the grey-green spikes were used widely in medicine at one time. The foxglove too was used extensively in medicine for the drug digitalin, extracted from its leaves, helps in the treatment of heart disorders.

Below, main picture: Wild Thyme. Inset: Sundew. Right: Herb Robert. Opposite, top: Bird's-Foot Trefoil. Opposite, bottom left: Foxgloves. Opposite, bottom right: Cowslips

North Tynedale and Redesdale

No fre brother of this Fellyshype shall, from hensfourthe, take no apprentice, to serve in this Fellyshype of non suche as is or shalbe borne or brought up in Tyndall, Ryddisdall or anye other suche lycke places; in payne of £20.

Newcastle Merchant
Adventurers (1554)

The valleys of the North Tyne and Rede are always associated in people's minds with the stormy days of Border strife when England and Scotland were constantly at war and people on either side of the Border at each others' throats. The inhabitants of the two valleys gained a reputation for lawlessness, dishonesty, intemperance and ungodly habits and were noted (and valued) for their fighting qualities. Yet this reputation was, to some extent, foisted upon them for they are remote areas of England lying on the very border with Scotland. For a long time it was a moot point whether they would end up as English or Scottish possessions. It is the use to which these valleys were put – as buffer zones by the English, that resulted in time in the unenviable reputation their inhabitants undoubtedly had.

The two valleys are formed by the River North Tyne rising near Deadwater Fell and by its tributary, the Rede, which rises on Carter Fell. Each valley provides good arable land and pasture while, as the land gains height each side of the rivers and where it is not forest, heather moorland predominates. Wild goats roam on Kielder Moor; birds of prey hover above the fells seeking larger prey than the emperor moth which anyone walking across the heather is quite likely to catch sight of, or see their large green caterpillars that the cuckoo likes so much. Shooting butts declare the presence of grouse on the hills while partridges are coming back into their own on the valley floors. The rivers are still the haunt of otters and have increasingly become home to wild mink. A number of heronries exist in the area and it is sad that the otter and heron have been blamed by anglers for destroying the fish population and in turn have been, or are still being, destroyed for that reason.

Left: Near Donkleywood. Above left: River North Tyne, Ridley Stokoe. Top right: Wild Goat. Bottom right: Otter

Sheep-farming is the main industry of the valleys, the black-face breed being the most common; in fact the town of Bellingham annually hosts the Black-faced Sheep Breeders' Ball.

There are deposits of coal, lime and iron ore within the valleys which at various times have been worked commercially; coal is still mined in the North Tyne Valley.

Farming and forestry have destroyed most of the ancient settlements in the two valleys. It is quite certain, however, that by the time the Romans arrived in Redesdale the main occupation of the local people was subsistence farming.

The Romans in Redesdale

Under the Romans the Britons were forced to step up production because cereal for food and animals' hides for uniforms, boots and tents of the occupying army were exacted from them. Redesdale was occupied in strength with Dere Street as the major communication link between north and south. It says much for Agricola that this road remained the major link into Scotland for another 1600 years. It carries much of the modern A68 now, and the Roman milestone on the left of the road as it breasts the hill going north from West Woodburn is an enduring sign of Agricola's time.

Two large forts, each housing 1000 cavalry, were established at Risingham (Habitancum) and High Rochester (Bremenium). In addition there were at least fourteen camps and two minor forts

Left: River North Tyne, Ridge End. Above: Roman milestone, Corsenside, Redesdale

along the line of the road. Many of these would be temporary housing for the road-builders; but some would be used for troops which makes a nice comparison between Redesdale then and now. Agricola in AD 78 saw Redesdale as an ideal base for his army of occupation. Winston Churchill, staying with Lord Redesdale for a shooting party in 1910, saw the Otterburn moors as an excellent artillery range. In 1911 the War Office purchased the Featherwood Estate from Lord Redesdale and so the Redesdale All Arms Training Area was started. Now it covers 22,663 hectares in Redesdale and Coquetdale.

Towers, Peles and Bastles

By the time the Normans conquered England two significant changes had taken place. First, Christianity had been introduced: two churches, dedicated to St Cuthbert, built on the present sites at Bellingham and Elsdon, pre-date the Conquest. Secondly, Redesdale had been made, and Tynedale was to be made, a 'liberty' so that both valleys became subject to local law rather than the law of the land. The motte and bailey castles at Elsdon and Wark on Tyne, both heads of their respective liberties, were built shortly after the Conquest. Dally Castle and Tarset Hall in North Tynedale were built of stone in the succeeding centuries.

The towers, peles and bastles, in that order, that were built subsequently, resulted from the disorder into which Edward I's war against Scotland threw the whole of the Border region. In the twenty years of official hostilities fierce national hatred on either side of the border, which had never existed before, sprang up between rival barons; when their power became broken this degenerated into clan feuds, thieving and murder. The towers at Hesleyside, in North Tynedale, and at Troughend and Otterburn (now the Otterburn Tower Hotel), at Corsenside and Elsdon where the Vicar's Pele gave protection to the people of that lonely outpost, were built by 1415.

The final phase of fortified building, and the one most peculiar to Northumberland, came about in the sixteenth century when lawlessness was at its height. The Government ordered that, as it was not possible to provide the men to protect the borderers, they must look to their own defences. As well as digging

Below: Black Middens Bastle. Opposite, top: Gatehouse, North Bastle. Opposite, bottom: Drystone wall and meadow, North Tyne

ditches and planting hedges across well-known routes, the headmen of the villages should build their own fortified houses, of stone, to protect both themselves and their cattle. Nothing much was done about the ditches and hedges; presumably these would only make it as difficult for the English as for the Scots. The defensible houses were, however, built and are now known as 'bastle houses'.

Bastle houses exist only within a narrow belt of land twenty miles wide along the length of the Border and nowhere else in England. The style throughout is very similar; thirty-five feet by twenty-five feet with four-foot or so thick walls, two floors and a steeply pitched roof with gable-ends. The roof was often covered with heather or turfs, more rarely in stone slates. The ground floor, ventilated by narrow slits and entered only by a stoutly barred door in one gable-end, was for the stock, while the family living quarters were above, reached from the outside by a removable ladder or, from inside, by a spiral staircase or ladder. At least if a bastle was raided it was going to take some time for the defenders to be smoked out and by that time help would have arrived from a neighbouring bastle, for these

tended to be built in groups or within sight of each other.

Of those that have survived many now have stone steps leading outside to the upper floor; these were a later addition when times were peaceful, but the houses continued to be occupied. Most are now merely part of a farm's outbuildings. In North Tynedale there are the remains of fifteen bastles, eight of them in Tarset alone. Black Middens has recently been restored by English Heritage. Gatehouse, privately owned, is in very good repair. In Redesdale there are at least eleven bastles of which High Rochester is a good example, while in the deserted village of Evistones the uses to which such buildings are now put can be seen.

There is a whole folklore about the Border Troubles, a euphemism that hardly conjures up the horrors of the times. The women were no less formidable than the men. The Lady of Hesleyside, in the days before Hesleyside was the beautiful mansion it is now, was supposed to have presented a spur on a salver in place of meat when the larder was bare – a sign for her men to go on another raid.

The romance of the Border, which undoubtedly surrounds this murky period, is enhanced by

the Border Ballads, handed down orally by the shepherds and their families and collected by Sir Walter Scott. He was enthralled by them and passed them on in written form to the rest of the world. Sir Philip Sydney, much earlier, was equally enthralled: 'I never heard the olde song of Percy and Douglas that I found not my heart moved more than with a trumpet.' This was the Battle of Otterburn, fought in 1388 by the light of a thin moon. Douglas was killed and Percy (Shakespeare's Hotspur) was captured. A battle fought by heroes it may have been, but it is just one example of the hatred and rivalry between Border barons that did so much to prolong the strife and ultimately degrade the standard of life of their people. The ballad starts very sweetly:

Yt fell about the Lammas tyde,
When husbandes win their haye,

then it goes on:

The dowtye Douglasse bound him
to ryde,
yn Yngland to take a praye.

A hundred Scots were killed, over 1000 English were taken or killed; the dead were buried in a mass grave in Elsdon churchyard. Percy's Cross, one and a half miles north of Otterburn, and the Battle Seat at Bennetsfield, glorify the battle. Other ballads tell a different story of the times; of murder, 'The Death of Parcy Reed', and of sorrow, 'The Lament of the Border Widow'.

It took a long time for Redesdale and North Tynedale to recover from these times. When the Duke of Northumberland visited Kielder in 1765 he observed that the women had no other dress than a bed-gown and petticoat; the men, his tenants, sang a wild chorus consisting largely of the words 'Ourina, Ourina, Ourina'.

Afforestation
New roads, agricultural improvements and local industries all contributed to the improvement of life in the two valleys. The largest undertaking, however, has occurred this century and has caused the most dramatic change of landscape. Kielder Forest, the vast complex of tightly packed spruce, now stretches from the mosses north of Hadrian's Wall Area right up to Redesdale. The Forest, divided into Wark, Kielder, Falstone and Redesdale forests, covers 40,176 hectares of land. A forest drive between Byrness and Kielder gives motorists access to one part of the forest where roe deer or the red squirrel might be seen.

Kielder Water
The largest man-made lake in Europe, this reservoir is the newest addition to North Tynedale and provides opportunities

for boating, sailing, water-skiing, canoeing and fishing. Tower Knowe Information Centre is run jointly by the Northumbrian Water Authority and the National Park.

Falstone and the Shepherds' Art

Falstone lies just south of Kielder Dam and the boundary of the National Park. A typical Border village, it has its annual Border Shepherds Show. Pens of sheep, hound trails, sheep-dog trials, terrier and hound classes provide an afternoon of entertainment and interest. In the industrial tent, apart from the array of vegetables, home baking, flowers and handi-crafts, there is always a grand show of dressed sticks. This art has been practised of old among the Border shepherds in the long

all manner of people. Ram's horns are hard to come by. So are the shanks; some people say that they should be cut only when the sap is dormant; others say the only time to cut one is when you see one.

Elsdon

The Mote Hills, St Cuthbert's Church, Pele Tower and the green with the Georgian houses around it show Elsdon's impor-

tance in earlier times. One road leading from the village traverses the Grasslees Valley going into Coquetdale. It passes Billsmoor deer park and also some of the best fragments of the ancient forest cover of Northumberland. The National Park has management agreements with the owners of some of the woodland to help conserve and regenerate not only an important wildlife habitat, but part of our heritage.

winter evenings. A horn, preferably a ram's, is heated over a low flame and bent slowly, inch by inch, into the shape of a walking-stick or crook handle. This is then set on to a wooden shank, hazel, ash, blackthorn or holly, and then smoothed and polished to a perfect finish. These sticks, crooks, leg cleeks, mart sticks, were the shepherd's tools when working his sheep; they still are, but they made stick-dressing an art form and now it is practised by

Above, main picture: Kielder Water. Inset: Kielder Dam. Left: Stick dressing. Top right: Grasslees Valley. Centre right: Rock Rose, Grasslees. Right: St Cuthbert's Church and fourteenth-century pele tower, Elsdon

Upper Coquetdale and the Simonsides

The Coquet for ever! The Coquet
  for aye!
The Coquet, the King o' the stream
  an' the brae.
Frae his high mountain to his bed
  in the sea –
Oh! where shall we find such a
  River as he?

The Coquet provides the strongest contrast between the desolate moors where its headwaters lie on the Scottish border, and the many villages it passes in increasingly fertile farmland through which it flows until it reaches the sea at Warkworth. The moors around the head of the river were debatable land for long enough; both Scotland and England laid claim to pieces of it as late as the nineteenth century. The only debatable point about the Coquet is whether or not it is

the best trout river in the county. Its devotees say it is and the number of Coquetdale fishing songs add their chorus to the claim. Possibly the best advertisement for its excellence is the complaint of the old man in the last years of the nineteenth century whose theme was: 'There's no sic fishen in Coquet now as when I was a lad. It was nowse then but to fling in an' pull oot by tweeses and threeses, if ye had as many hooks on, but now a body may keep threshin at the watter aa' day atween Hallysteun and Weldon an' hardly catch three dozen . . .'. Permits for salmon, migratory fish and trout on the Coquet at Rothbury and Thropton are obtainable now from The Fishing Tackle Shop, High Street, Rothbury.

The Simonside and Harbottle Hills

South of the River Coquet the Simonside Hills provide the strongest contrast between the green valley below and the black of the heather moors on the steep slopes. The sandstone beds of the Simonsides were laid down millions of years ago as sand was washed down by a huge river, considerably larger than the Mississippi, which flowed across what is now the North Sea and much of North West Europe. Simonside, at 429 metres, is the highest point of the hills in which the underlying sandstone reaches a depth of more than 600 metres. The upper beds of sandstone on the hills are more coarsely grained than those at lower levels and are known as Rothbury Grit. This was once quarried for millstones.

Above left: Shillmoor Farm. Left: Millstones at Harbottle Crags. Above: Holystone Grange and River Coquet. Right: Sandy Crags and Simonside Hills

1

3

4

2

5

6

9

7   8

Birds

The diversity of land through which the Coquet flows makes Coquetdale an excellent centre for the bird-watcher. Anyone walking the moors has a good chance of seeing some of the larger birds of prey as well as plover, curlew and dunlin. The broad loops of the Lower Coquet and the fertile valley floor provide a haven for oystercatchers, sandpipers, dippers, wagtails, martins and peewits. In winter Scandinavian migrants like the redwing and fieldfare arrive to boost the bird population. The Ryton Sand and Gravel Group at Caistron near Hepple, have made a Nature Reserve in the unlikely environment of a gravel extraction plant. This has provided sanctuary at some time to virtually every bird species found in Coquetdale. Visits can be arranged to the Reserve through the Caistron Manager, telephone Rothbury 40226.

1 Sand Martin. 2 Dunlin. 3 Grey Wagtails. 4 Sparrow Hawk. 5 Hen Peregrine. 6 Oystercatcher. 7 Dipper. 8 Common Sandpiper. 9 Hen Merlin

Ancient Settlements

A series of hill-forts surrounds Rothbury and cap many of the hills throughout the region. One of the most accessible and impressive is Lordenshaws Hill-Fort on the east side of the Simonside Hills. Lying at the junction of four ancient trackways this Iron Age fort covers an area of 137 metres in diameter. There are no signs of cultivation so it seems likely that the people who lived here reared cattle. A number of cairns and an open cist in which a person may attempt the crouched up burial position, are evidence of a long period of occupation.

Rock Carvings

Cup and ring marked stones found in this area and on the sandstone ridge east of the Cheviots, while found elsewhere in the upland parts of Britain, form a rich feature of the Northumbrian landscape. They are the great mystery, being flat rocks carved with curious cup-like hollows usually encircled by concentric rings which, in turn, are often joined by straight grooves. Their meaning is unknown. They were probably Early Bronze Age phenomena and probably had a religious significance; or they may have been maps, fertility symbols or even represent games people played. The rock carvings on Garleigh Moor, in close association with the Lorden-

shaws Camp, make this small area of the Simonsides of great interest.

Later Settlements

The Border Troubles have been mentioned earlier, but Coquetdale was no less prone to them than other parts of Northumberland. The only difference between Coquetdale and Redesdale seems to have been that the people of Coquetdale were more honest and better able to be governed.

Tosson Tower was a fifteenth-century stronghold built to guard the passes south from Coquetdale over the Simonside range. Despite its strength — forty-two feet by thirty-six feet with walls nine feet thick — it was already in

a state of disrepair by 1541, in company with the whole line of towers extending from Harbottle to Warkworth and built against the incursions of the Scots. Opposite the tower is the house which used to be the Royal George Inn; presumably this hostelry was named some time after 1715. In that year the gentlemen of Coquetdale mustered on Plainfield Moor, north of Hepple, when they joined the Earl of Derwentwater in the First Jacobite Rebellion. Much of the Simonside Hills were included in the Forest of Rothbury; now a large area is covered with the conifer plantations of Harbottle Forest.

Holystone was of much greater importance in ancient and

medieval times. Traces of early British settlements surround the village. The Roman road connecting Bremenium in Redesdale with the Devil's Causeway near Thrunton in Coquetdale, passes close to the village, and the path to the Lady's Well or Holywell is part of this track. The Holywell is a natural spring, said to discharge 500 gallons of water a minute which feeds into a stone-lined well in a grove of trees. It is at this well that the missionary Paulinus, Archbishop of York, is said to have baptised 3000 converts at Easter, 627, after he had introduced Christianity into Northumberland. It was a busy time for him because on the same date he is supposed to have baptised several hundred people at Walltown, near Hadrian's Wall and yet another 2000 in the River Glen near Yeavering Bell.

Just south of the village is Holystone Grange, once called Dues Hill or Woodhouse Grange. This house was much enlarged in 1897 and thousands of trees planted in the grounds. Dues Hill Bastle, with 1602 carved on its lintel, is close to the Grange and is one of the best preserved of these defensible farmhouses. The Five Kings, the remnants of a stone circle of the Bronze Age, is nearby.

Harbottle. The best view of this village is obtained from the Drake Stone on the Harbottle Crags from where the change of course that the Coquet has taken can be seen. Harbottle was important before the Conquest as it was a royal fortress in Saxon times. In the twelfth century the capital of Redesdale was moved from Elsdon to Harbottle and a motte and bailey castle was built soon after 1157. A stone castle soon replaced the original wooden tower and was large enough to house 100 horsemen for the Keeper of Redesdale. The local population was kept in hand by

the presence of pillory and stocks, prison and gallows – on Gallows Edge. Most of the stone from the castle, which was one of the largest in the county, was used to build the modern Harbottle Castle; the old one was too far gone for repair by 1604.

The modern village of Harbottle lies in the shelter of the castle mound, with far fewer houses and inhabitants now than when the Umfravilles were Lords of Redesdale and built their stronghold. The lack of overhead wires here does not denote the absence of modern facilities; a National Park initiative got telephone and electricity cables

Above left: Prehistoric carved rock, Garleigh Moor. Left: Tosson Tower. Top right: The Lady's Well, Holystone. Centre right: Harbottle Castle and village. Right: Harbottle village

placed underground to enhance the attractiveness of the village.

About a mile north of Harbottle is an Information Centre run jointly by the Northumberland Wildlife Trust and the National Park. A track from the centre goes up to Harbottle Crags, the Drake Stone and Harbottle Lough, a small tarn where there used to be a large heronry. The Wildlife Trust runs a permanent nature trail along the track.

Alwinton is famous for its show. Nearly every village in Northumberland has an annual show, but Alwinton's is the last every year of the Border shepherd shows. Held on the second Saturday of October, Alwinton attracts farmers and shepherds from all over the Border to show the best of their stock. Scottish black-face and cheviots are the main breeds paraded and the

pedigree dogs at Cruft's have no more care lavished on their appearance than these sheep. The black-face is fairly easy. Excess hair is trimmed off round the neck, ears and face, and around the tops of the legs. The horns are brushed clean with a wire brush before being, if necessary, filed, sand-papered and, in cases of extreme need, heated and bent to a better angle. The sheep is then dipped in a shampoo, but the fleece is not brushed when dry because that would take the purl (kink) out of it. The tail, however, is brushed and, if necessary, trimmed. The last thing before the show is to oil the sheep's horns and also its face to bring out the sheen on its black facial hair in such contrast to its now creamy-white body. The cheviot has no horns but it takes much longer to prepare. The fleece must first be teased out and then clipped perfectly flat all over, including the underneath. This is known as 'blocking out'. The next stage, probably a day or so later, is to dip the sheep – no colourants may be added but proprietary brands of shampoo are available for the wash. When dry the fleece is teased out again and further levelling off takes place. The shape of the animal should now

be a perfect rectangle as far as the fleece is concerned, the flatter the better. Any long hairs must also be trimmed off the tail. The final stage is to whiten the sheep's face with zinc oxide powder having first washed it with soap and water. As a last resort, should the sheep get a dirty mark on its face prior to entering the show pen, a dusting of baby powder can hide it.

Farming

Sheep-farming has formed the staple of employment in these hills for hundreds of years and still does. The Monks of Newminster were granted large tracts of grazing land in Kidland as early as the twelfth century. Clennell Street runs from Clennel, north of Alwinton, to Cocklawfoot in Scotland. Even in this century the flocks of sheep driven down the 'street' were so large that five gates had to be opened at once in the fence between Bloodybush Edge and Yarnspath Law to allow them to pass.

Above: Upper Coquet Valley and Alwinton Show. Above left: Dressing sheep for Alwinton Show. Opposite, top: Cotton-grass. Opposite, bottom: Windy Gyle

The Cheviots

When the sea covered the land over 300 million years ago Cheviot remained high above it, an active volcano. The sea floor had emerged as dry land in the region of the Scottish border and on to this the Cheviot volcano erupted flinging ashes thousands of feet into the air which accumulated on the land to a depth of perhaps 150 feet. To this was added the outpourings of a continuous lava flow which covered an area of 230 square miles. The pinkish rocks surrounding Cheviot are Andesite deposits from the volcano. The granite core of Cheviot itself was intruded at a later stage. Stone quarried at Biddlestone is porphyrite, a volcanic rock pushed up through the Andesite, used to line The Mall in London – a red carpet to the gates of Buckingham Palace. The soft sandstone with cementstones and shales, were formed from the sediments deposited in the delta of an enormous river which flowed from what is now Scandinavia into the sea south of the Cheviot. Volcanic activity formed the

structure of the Cheviot, ice then shaped it, smoothing the hills into rounded tops and widening the deep valleys through which the burns now flow.)

Cheviot stands 815 metres high, its top covered by a four metre layer of boggy peat. Daniel Defoe, making his ascent of Cheviot, described the summit as a flat area of about half a mile in diameter with a large pond in the middle. The damp conditions that now prevail support cloudberry, cotton-grass and sphagnum.

Cheviot's whaleback shape can be seen from great distances, especially when capped with snow. More distinctive, although lower, is Hedgehope Hill's conical shape at 714 metres. Early every summer these lonely hills are invaded by about 200 people taking part in the seventeen-mile Chevy Chase.

Farming

The farms in the Cheviots are large; the average holding is about 1000 hectares, although

some are in excess of 4000 hectares, mainly carrying sheep with some hill cattle. The pattern of managing the stock has not altered dramatically over centuries. Sheep are hefted on to the land; it is their home ground, so if a farm is sold the sheep are sold with it. The main breeds are cheviots and mules, these being a cross between the Scottish black-face and a blue-faced Leicester ram. On the highest land Scottish black-face and swaledales are used because of their hardiness. Most of the lambs are still sold at the Wooler Auction Mart each autumn for fattening on lowland farms. The cattle are beef breeds, Angus or Hereford crosses for the most part but the tendency has increasingly been to put suckler cows to a Charolais or Limousin bull although Hereford bulls are still used. In lowland farming areas the ratio of sheep to land is four sheep to an acre; in the Cheviots it is one sheep to an acre because the land is unable to support more.

Ancient Settlements

The Cheviot Hills began to be settled during the Bronze Age, after 2000 BC and the large number of settlements, forts, cultivation terraces and cairns bears testament to the presence of these early people and their successors in the Iron Age and Romano-British period.

Bronze Age people were farmers, but during the Bronze Age the climate was better and even with their rudimentary tools, they were able to grow crops of barley and wheat. The small cairns found on land surrounding the unenclosed Bronze Age settlement on Langlee Crags suggest that land was cleared of stone purely for the purpose of growing crops.

The development of hill forts took place later in the Iron Age, about 500 BC when rival tribes or groups of people consolidated

Above right: Sheep in the Cheviot Hills. Far right: Ilderton Dod, Iron Age hill-fort. Right: Charolais and Simmenthal Bulls

their territory. A change in climate had reduced the area of useful agricultural land so that the pattern had changed from arable to stock raising. Most of the hill forts in the Cheviots are quite small.

Yeavering Bell is the most important of all the hill-forts in Northumberland. Its summit, encircled by a single stone rampart and ditch, enclosing at least 130 huts, was almost certainly an important tribal centre of the Votadini. For years it was thought that this was the capital of Edwin of Northumbria. However the site of Ad Gefrin, Edwin's palace, has now been determined as being at the foot of Yeavering Bell. A roadside monument marks the

Left, main picture: The solitude of the Cheviot Hills. Inset: Bog Rosemary. Below left: Yervering Bell (conical hill, centre right) from Weetwood. Below: Collingwood Oaks and College Valley

site. It was here in the River Glen that Paulinus baptised converts to Christianity in 627. As a postscript to the introduction of Christianity to Northumbria, there is a curious carving in the church at Kirk Newton, about half a mile north of Ad Gefrin. The sculpture celebrates the Adoration of the Magi. Presumably the sculptor was a local man; he dressed his Magi in kilts.

The Forest of Cheviot and The Collingwood Oaks

The ancient forest cover of Northumberland was established while Britain was still joined to the continent of Europe. In turn willow, birch, pine, oak, alder and ash covered much of the land and the few fragments which exist today are in places too inaccessible for man to have been bothered about cutting them. For this he began to do from the Stone Age onwards. After the Conquest forests were to some extent protected as hunting grounds where the birds and beasts dwelt in the safe protection of the king 'for his delight and pleasure'; red deer and roe, wild boar and wolves still inhabited the wild wood. The Forest of Cheviot was described in 1541 as being The Cheviot itself and generally as the land lying between the head of Elterburn and the hanging stone, east and west, and the border with Scotland on the north and the College Valley in the south. At that time, when cross border raiding was at its height, the Scots were firmly blamed for the disappearance of woodland; 'The Scottes as well by nighte time secretely as upon the daie tyme with more force, do come into the said forrest of Cheviott . . . and steale and carrye awaie much of the said wood whyche ys to them a greatt proffyte for the maynten'aunce of their houses and buildings.' Since the English, over a much longer period, did much the same, it is hardly surprising there is so little left. Remnants exist, however, upon most of the steep burnsides that cut into the Cheviots and are a habitat for primroses, bluebells and wood sorrel.

A much later addition to the woodland cover of the area are the Collingwood Oaks. Admiral Collingwood inherited the Hethpool Estate through his wife. A

Above, main picture: Housey Crags, Cheviot Hills. Inset: Common Primrose

major preoccupation of his in the short periods he was at home was to collect acorns and plant them wherever he could so that they would grow into fine timber for his beloved navy. He planted the grove of oaks on Hethpool Bell for this reason. Management of them with the agreement of the present owner was taken over by the National Park in 1980. The fence was erected to keep out cattle and prevent grazing which destroys young seedlings.

In the vicinity of the Collingwood Oaks, in early summer, the wild goats come down from the high hills for the birth of their young. These shaggy grey and black creatures are probably descended from the goats kept as stock in medieval times which periodically escaped and formed into herds. Their long black horns can make a very nice stick handle.

Roads and Whisky Smuggling

Until the eighteenth century there were no good roads in the Cheviot area. Dere Street was the major crossing into Scotland. There were other, less well defined routes used by the drovers; Clennell Street, was one. The Salter's Road which goes from Alnham across the lower stretches of the Cheviots to Uswayford and the Border was another.

The Satter's Road was probably an important track in prehistoric times, passing the hillfort at Alnham. In medieval times it was used by trains of packhorses taking salt from the saltpans on the Northumbrian coast into Scotland. It was probably also used by smugglers because it passes close to Rory's Still at Davidson's Linn on the Usway Burn. The most famous of the several distillers was Black Rory and the best preserved of the stills is Rory's Still.

The Cheviot Valleys

Valleys cut into the Cheviots from the south, east and north; each is served by a road, usually single track with passing places, which leads to a single, isolated farm. Public rights of way criss-cross the hills between the valleys which, with the superb scenery, richness of wildlife and superabundant reminders of the past, make excellent walking country. Three valleys, however, are more easily accessible than the others; in two of them access agreements exist between the National Park and the landowners; the third is a privately owned estate which has a system of permits for cars.

The Breamish Valley. Access Land is on the haughs between Brandon and Ingram Bridge and between Bulby's Wood and

Opposite: 1 Cranberry. 2 Cloudberry. 3 Bilberry. 4 Rock Rose and Lady's Bedstraw. 5 Tormentil. 6 Harebell. 7 Yellow Bedstraw

Plants

Grass is the predominant moorland cover in the Cheviots although heather covers some of the more peaty soils giving way to crowberry and bilberry in exposed areas. Sheep's fescue, bents and wavy hair grass cover much of the well-drained steep hillsides; the tiny blue-coloured milkwort, yellow tormentil and white-flowered heath bedstraw grow here, too. On the higher slopes mat grass predominates. This plant bleaches in summer giving a white look to large areas so that they have come to be called, locally, 'white lands'.

2

5

6

3

4

7

Peggy Bell's Bridge. This valley has been a favourite place for picnickers, sightseers and walkers especially since World War II. The hill-fort at Brough Law dominates the central part of the valley; at the head of it Linhope Spout provides a dramatic fall of water and the prehistoric village of Greaves Ash lies close by.

The Harthope Valley. Access Land lies between Carey Burn bridge and Hawsen Burn with a number of permissive paths giving access to the higher land on either side of the valley. Sir Walter Scott who stayed in the Harthope Valley for a holiday was very enthusiastic. 'Out of these brooks we pull trouts of half a yard in length. My uncle drinks the whey here as I do ever since I understood it was brought to his bedside at six every morning by a very pretty dairymaid.' He added that he could only write the

Below, main picture: The Cheviot Hills. Inset: Gorse. Opposite: The Harthope Burn

letter after shooting a crow to obtain a quill. If he had gone up to the moors he would surely have seen the merlin which favours the Cheviot area and nests on heathery ground of the less high hills. A stone circle on the Threestone Burn is quite close to Langlee Farm where Sir Walter stayed. Five stones remain standing out of an original thirteen, of which 'threestone' is probably a corruption.

The College Valley is owned by a charitable trust and access to it is limited to twelve cars a day, except for lambing time in April and May when no cars are permitted. Permits can be obtained, free, from the estate agents, John Sale & Partners, Glendale Road, Wooler. The head of this valley lies very close to the Border Line and it is in just such isolated places that the peregrine might be expected to be seen high in flight above the moors. The lower reaches of the College Burn are particularly welcoming; the mass of vivid yellow when the gorse flowers in June and which grows

in profusion along the burn will raise anyone's spirits.

Kilham Valley at the far north of the Park has no special access arrangements but the farmer, in co-operation with the National Park, has organised a Farm Trail on his land which is open throughout the summer. The farm now is famous for its herd of pure-bred Aberdeen Angus cattle. The views into Scotland from these hills show exactly why the English seized every opportunity to plunder into that forbidden territory. Kilham Farm in return received several unwelcome visits from the Scots who used to come into the valley from Yetholm Mains.

If you had traversed the National Park via the Pennine Way, the last forty kilometres of it would have given you some of the best views of the Cheviot Hills, a sense of history of the country as you walked along the Border fence and, above all, a feel of this most northerly National Park, the spaciousness of it and the room to breathe.